Pets and People

Eldonna L. Evertts/*Language Arts*
Bernard J. Weiss/*Linguistics and Reading*

Susan B. Cruikshank/*Reading and Language Arts*

Educational Consultants
Jack P. Henderson
Janet Sprout

Related Satellite Books
Lyman C. Hunt/*General Editor*

The Holt Basic Reading System

Level 5

HOLT, RINEHART AND WINSTON, PUBLISHERS
New York · Toronto · London · Sydney

ISBN 0-03-016986-0
7890 071 9876543

Acknowledgments:

Grateful acknowledgment is given to G. P. Putnam's Sons for "The Goldfish," from *Everything and Anything* by Dorothy Aldis. Copyright 1925, 1926, 1927 by Dorothy Aldis. Used by permission.

Art Credits:

Ethel Gold, pages 4–11
Betty Fraser, pages 12–20
Marilyn Lucey, page 21
Len Ebert, pages 22–29
Marilyn Bass Goldman, page 30
Arthur Friedman, page 31
Lorraine Fox, pages 32–40
Diane de Groat, pages 41, 52–61
Jack Endewelt, pages 42–51
Viewpoint Graphics, Inc., page 62

Cover design and illustration by Pellegrini, Kaestle & Gross, Inc.

Table of Contents

4

Stop Gus!

Gus ran into a big store.

Sandy ran into the store.

"Stop, Gus," she said.

Gus didn't stop.

A big boy saw Gus.

"Stop," the big boy said.
"Come here, dog."

Gus didn't stop.
He ran out.

Two girls saw Gus.

The girls ran to stop Gus.

Gus didn't stop.

A little boy saw Gus.

"Here, dog," said the little boy.
"Good dog.
See the cookies?"

Gus saw the cookies.

What did he do?

He ran to the little boy.

The big boy and the girls saw Gus.

What did they do?

They ran to Gus and the boy.

Sandy didn't stop Gus.

The big boy didn't stop Gus.

The two girls didn't stop Gus.

The cookies did!

What Can You Do with a Burro?

"Come and see my burro," said Pablo.

The boys and girls ran with Pablo.

They ran to see the burro.

"He is a good burro," said a boy.
"But what can you do with a burro?"

"Here," said Pablo.

"You can play with a burro."

Pablo ran up to the burro.

But the burro didn't play.

"The burro won't play," said a girl.

"What **can** you do with a burro?"

"You can do a trick," said Pablo.
"My burro will do a trick."

But the burro didn't do the trick.

"The burro won't play," said a boy.

"The burro won't do the trick.

What can you do with a burro?"

Pablo ran to the burro.

"You can love a burro," he said.

And he did!

Pablo Has a Donkey

—Nona Keen Duffy

Pablo has a donkey
His ears go floppy-flop!
It's hard to get him started,
It's hard to make him stop!

Pablo's beast is stubborn,
He balks at every hill,
At times he's very trying
But Pablo loves him still!

Swim Up!

"A kite!" said Sora.
"A kite like a goldfish!
Is the kite for me?
But who is it from?"

Sora saw a sign on the kite.

The sign said,

　　To Sora

　　From Big Brother

The kite was from Big Brother!

Big Brother was in Japan.

"Swim, goldfish," said Sora.

"Swim in the sky.

Swim up.

Swim up in the sky."

26

The goldfish went up.

Up and up it went.

And up went Sora!

"Good-by, house!" said Sora.

"Good-by, people!

My goldfish likes to swim up in the sky!"

"Do you see a house?" said Sora.

"It is a house," said the kite.
"A house in Japan!"

"Who is he?" said Sora.
"Is he my brother?
He is my brother!"

"Goldfish, what a trick!" said Sora.

"You can swim up from my house.

You can swim down to a house in Japan.

From my house to Japan!"

"What a kite!" said Big Brother.

"What a Sora!" said the kite.

The Goldfish

My darling little goldfish
Hasn't any toes;
He swims around without a sound
And bumps his hungry nose.

He can't get out to play with me,
Nor I get in to him,
Although I say: "Come out and play,"
And he—"Come in and swim."

—Dorothy Aldis

Making New Words

ran	it	did	up	Ben
rag	if	dig	us	bed

Gus ran with the rag.

Ben went to bed.

See us up here.

Did Rex like to dig?

Jill will read the book if she likes it.

Shep, the Sheep Dog

Shep was a sheep dog.

He was a good sheep dog.

"Come here, Shep!" said Tim.

Shep came.

"Where is my little sheep?" said Tim.

"Go find it, Shep."

Shep went to find the little sheep.

He saw the little sheep.

The sheep ran and ran.

Shep ran and ran.

The little sheep came to some water.

The little sheep went into the water.

Shep came to the water.

He went in to get the sheep.

Tim ran to find Shep.

Shep was in the water.

The little sheep was in the water.

"Come on out, Shep," said Tim.

"Make the little sheep come out."

The little sheep came out.

Shep came out.

"Good dog," said Tim.

"You are a good sheep dog."

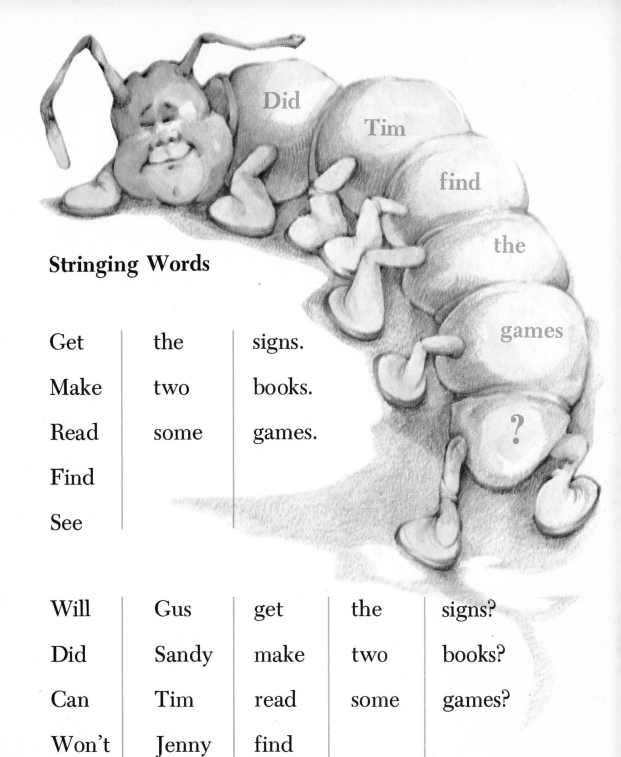

Did Tim find the games ?

Stringing Words

Get	the	signs.
Make	two	books.
Read	some	games.
Find		
See		

Will	Gus	get	the	signs?
Did	Sandy	make	two	books?
Can	Tim	read	some	games?
Won't	Jenny	find		
		see		

Bluebell, the Cow

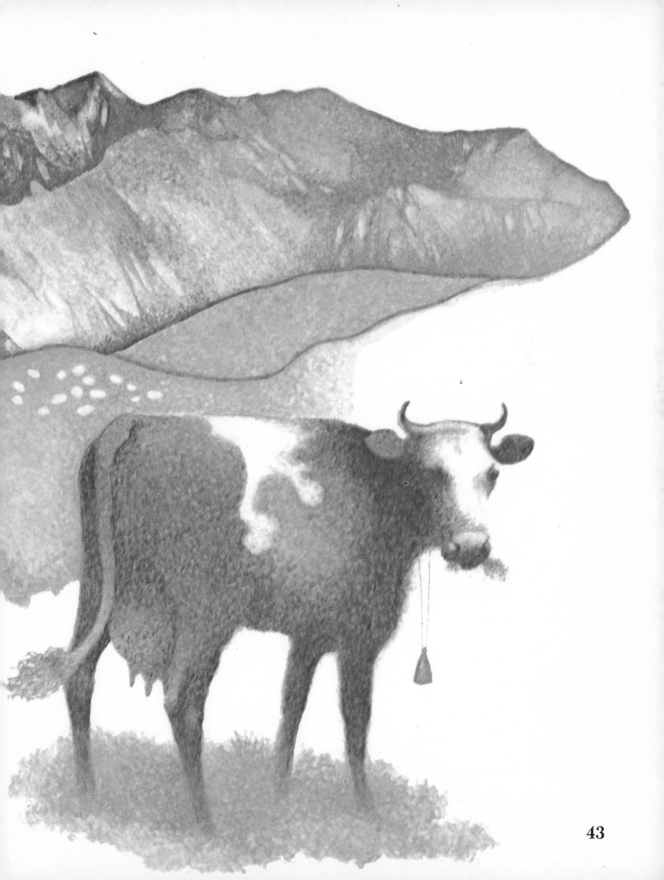

A little boy was in the house.

"I want to play," he said.

"I will get my brother."

The little boy ran to get his brother.

"Play with me," said the little boy.

"No," said his brother.
"I want to play with my dog."

The little boy ran to his sister.

"Will you play with me?" he asked.

"No," said his sister.

"I want to read my book."

"What can I do?" asked the little boy.

The little boy saw Bluebell.

He ran to the cow.

"I will make Bluebell play," he said.

And up he went.

"Get up, Bluebell," said the boy.

"Get up and play with me.

Go, Bluebell, go."

The boy didn't make Bluebell go.

"Here comes my sister," said the boy.

"She will make you go."

"Come down," said his sister.

"You won't make the cow go."

"What can she do?" asked the boy.

"See," said the girl.

"Here is what a cow can do."

The Cow

The friendly cow all red and white,
I love with all my heart:
She gives me cream
    with all her might,
To eat with apple tart.

—Robert Louis Stevenson

Who Is It?

A little girl went to see Kolo.
She went to his house.

"Kolo, Kolo," she said.
"Come out and play."

"Who is it?" asked someone.

"It's Neko," said the girl.
"I want to play with Kolo."

"Who is it?" asked someone again.

"Neko," said the girl.

"I want Kolo to come out."

"Who is it?" asked someone.

"It's Neko," said the girl again.

"Will you get Kolo?
I want to play with Kolo."

Neko saw Kolo come to the house.

"Here you are," said Neko.
"I want you to come and play.
Who is in the house?"

"No one is in the house," said Kolo.

"Someone asked, 'Who is it?'
Someone **is** in the house," said Neko.

59

"Come with me," said Kolo.

"You will see who it is."

Kolo and Neko went into the house,

"Someone **is** here," said Kolo.

"And here he **is**!"

Putting Words Together

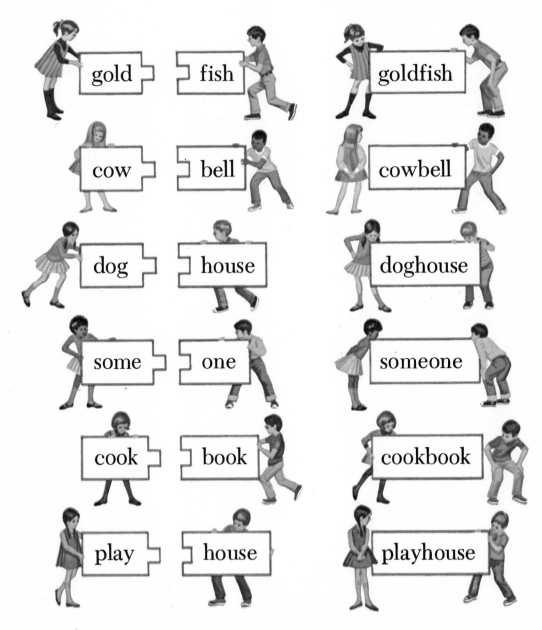

gold	fish	goldfish
cow	bell	cowbell
dog	house	doghouse
some	one	someone
cook	book	cookbook
play	house	playhouse

Stringing Words

Tim The boy He	likes	games.
Jenny The girl She	makes	cookies.
Jim and Dan The boys They	see	someone.
Jill and Sandy The girls They	play	here.

New Words

The words listed beside the page numbers below are introduced in *Pets and People*, Level 5 in THE HOLT BASIC READING SYSTEM.

5. stop
Gus

6. ran
Sandy
didn't

7. saw
he

13. can
with
burro

14. my
Pablo

15. but

17. won't

18. will

20. love

23. swim

24. kite
Sora
goldfish
from

25. brother
was
Japan

26. sky

27. went

33. Shep
sheep

35. Tim
came

37. water
get

42. Bluebell
cow

44. I
want
his

45. no

46. sister
asked

54. Kolo

55. it's
Neko

56. again